MznLnx

Missing Links Exam Preps

Exam Prep for

Fiscal Administration

Mikesell, 7th Edition

The MznLnx Exam Prep is your link from the texbook and lecture to your exams.
The MznLnx Exam Preps are unauthorized and comprehensive reviews of your textbooks.

All material provided by MznLnx and Rico Publications (c) 2010
Textbook publishers and textbook authors do not particpate in or contribute to these reviews.

MznLnx

Rico Publications

Exam Prep for Fiscal Administration
7th Edition
Mikesell

Publisher: Raymond Houge
Assistant Editor: Michael Rouger
Text and Cover Designer: Lisa Buckner
Marketing Manager: Sara Swagger
Project Manager, Editorial Production: Jerry Emerson
Art Director: Vernon Lowerui

Product Manager: Dave Mason
Editorial Assitant: Rachel Guzmanji
Pedagogy: Debra Long
Cover Image: Jim Reed/Getty Images
Text and Cover Printer: City Printing, Inc.
Compositor: Media Mix, Inc.

(c) 2010 Rico Publications
ALL RIGHTS RESERVED. No part of this work covered by the copyright may be reproduced or used in any form or by an means--graphic, electronic, or mechanical, including photocopying, recording, taping, Web distribution, information storage, and retrieval systems, or in any other manner--without the written permission of the publisher.

Printed in the United States
ISBN:

For more information about our products, contact us at:
Dave.Mason@RicoPublications.com

For permission to use material from this text or product, submit a request online to:
Dave.Mason@RicoPublications.com

Contents

CHAPTER 1
Fundamental Principles of Public Finance — 1

CHAPTER 2
The Logic of the Budget Process — 3

CHAPTER 3
Budget Structures and Institutions: Federal and State-Local — 7

CHAPTER 4
Budget Methods and Practices — 12

CHAPTER 5
Budget Classifications and Reform — 17

CHAPTER 6
Capital Budgeting, Public Infrastructure Investment, and Project Evaluation — 21

CHAPTER 7
Taxation: Criteria for Evaluating Revenue Options — 28

CHAPTER 8
Major Tax Structures: Income Taxes — 32

CHAPTER 9
Major Tax Structures: Taxes on Goods and Services — 40

CHAPTER 10
Major Tax Structures: Property Taxes — 43

CHAPTER 11
Revenue from User Fees, User Charges, and Sales by Public Monopolies — 46

CHAPTER 12
Collecting Taxes — 49

CHAPTER 13
Revenue Forecasts, Revenue Estimates, and Tax Expenditure Budgets — 51

CHAPTER 14
Intergovernmental Fiscal Relations: Diversity and Coordination — 55

CHAPTER 15
Debt Administration — 57

CHAPTER 16
Managing Funds: Cash Management and Employee Retirement Funds — 62

ANSWER KEY — 69

TO THE STUDENT

COMPREHENSIVE

The *MznLnx* Exam Prep series is designed to help you pass your exams. Editors at MznLnx review your textbooks and then prepare these practice exams to help you master the textbook material. Unlike study guides, workbooks, and practice tests provided by the texbook publisher and textbook authors, *MznLnx* gives you **all** of the material in each chapter in exam form, not just samples, so you can be sure to nail your exam.

MECHANICAL

The MznLnx Exam Prep series creates exams that will help you learn the subject matter as well as test you on your understanding. Each question is designed to help you master the concept. Just working through the exams, you gain an understanding of the subject--its a simple mechanical process that produces success.

INTEGRATED STUDY GUIDE AND REVIEW

MznLnx is not just a set of exams designed to test you, its also a comprehensive review of the subject content. Each exam question is also a review of the concept, making sure that you will get the answer correct without having to go to other sources of material. You learn as you go! Its the easiest way to pass an exam.

HUMOR

Studying can be tedious and dry. MznLnx's instructional design includes moderate humor within the exam questions on occassion, to break the tedium and revitalize the brain

Chapter 1. Fundamental Principles of Public Finance

1. A _____ is any one of a variety of different systems, institutions, procedures, social relations and infrastructures whereby persons trade, and goods and services are exchanged, forming part of the economy. It is an arrangement that allows buyers and sellers to exchange things. _____s vary in size, range, geographic scale, location, types and variety of human communities, as well as the types of goods and services traded.
   a. Recession
   b. Market
   c. Market Failure
   d. Perfect competition

2. In economics, a _____ exists when the production or use of goods and services by the market is not efficient. That is, there exists another outcome where all involved can be made better off. A _____ can be viewed as a scenario where individuals' pursuit of pure self-interest leads to results that are not efficient - that can be improved upon from the societal point-of-view.
   a. Perfect competition
   b. Market failure
   c. Nominal value
   d. Recession

3. _____ is a common concept in economics, and gives rise to derived concepts such as consumer debt. Generally _____ is defined by opposition to production. But the precise definition can vary because different schools of economists define production quite differently.
   a. Mitigating Control
   b. Yield
   c. Starving the beast
   d. Consumption

4. In economics, a _____ is a good that is non-rivaled and non-excludable. This means, respectively, that consumption of the good by one individual does not reduce availability of the good for consumption by others; and that no one can be effectively excluded from using the good. In the real world, there may be no such thing as an absolutely non-rivaled and non-excludable good; but economists think that some goods approximate the concept closely enough for the analysis to be economically useful.
   a. Convertible bond
   b. Public good
   c. Net present value
   d. Velocity

5. In economics, an _____ or spillover of an economic transaction is an impact on a party that is not directly involved in the transaction. In such a case, prices do not reflect the full costs or benefits in production or consumption of a product or service. A positive impact is called an external benefit, while a negative impact is called an external cost.

a. Externality
b. AMEX
c. AIG
d. ABC Television Network

6. _____ in economics and business is the result of an exchange and from that trade we assign a numerical monetary value to a good, service or asset. If Alice trades Bob 4 apples for an orange, the _____ of an orange is 4 apples. Inversely, the _____ of an apple is 1/4 oranges.
   a. Discounts and allowances
   b. Transactional Net Margin Method
   c. Price
   d. Price discrimination

7. _____ is one of the four Ps of the marketing mix. The other three aspects are product, promotion, and place. It is also a key variable in microeconomic price allocation theory.
   a. Target costing
   b. Price
   c. Cost-plus pricing
   d. Pricing

8. _____ is the incidence or process of transferring ownership of a business, enterprise, agency or public service from the public sector (government) to the private sector (business.) In a broader sense, privatisation refers to transfer of any government function to the private sector including governmental functions like revenue collection and law enforcement.

The term 'Privatisation' also has been used to describe two unrelated transactions.

   a. BNSF Railway
   b. BMC Software, Inc.
   c. 3M Company
   d. Privatization

Chapter 2. The Logic of the Budget Process

1. Project _____: The project _____ is a prediction of the costs associated with a particular company project. These costs include labor, materials, and other related expenses. The project _____ is often broken down into specific tasks, with task _____s assigned to each.
   a. BMC Software, Inc.
   b. 3M Company
   c. BNSF Railway
   d. Budget

2. A _____ refers to the process by which governments create and approve a budget. Â· The Financial Service Department prepares worksheets to assist the department head in preparation of department budget estimates Â· The Administrator calls a meeting of managers and they present and discuss plans for the following yeare;s projected level of activity. Â· The managers can work with the Financial Services, or work alone to prepare an estimate for the departments coming year.
   a. BMC Software, Inc.
   b. 3M Company
   c. BNSF Railway
   d. Budget process

3. _____ are the income that is gained by governments because of taxation of the people.

Just as there are different types of tax, the form in which _____ is collected also differs; furthermore, the agency that collects the tax may not be part of central government, but may be an alternative third-party licenced to collect tax which they themselves will use. For example:

- In the UK, the DVLA collects road tax, which is then passed on the treasury.

_____s on purchases can come from two forms: 'tax' itself is a percentage of the price added to the purchase (such as sales tax in US states, or VAT in the UK), while 'duty' is a fixed amount added to the purchase price (such as is commonly found on cigarettes.) In order to calculate the total tax raised from these sales, we must work out the effective tax rate multiplied by the quantity supplied.

   a. Disposable income
   b. National War Tax Resistance Coordinating Committee
   c. Tax revenue
   d. Life insurance tax shelter

4. The general definition of an _____ is an evaluation of a person, organization, system, process, project or product. _____s are performed to ascertain the validity and reliability of information; also to provide an assessment of a system's internal control. The goal of an _____ is to express an opinion on the person/organization/system (etc) in question, under evaluation based on work done on a test basis.

a. Assurance service
b. Audit regime
c. Audit
d. Institute of Chartered Accountants of India

5. _____ is systematic determination of merit, worth, and significance of something or someone using criteria against a set of standards. _____ often is used to characterize and appraise subjects of interest in a wide range of human enterprises, including the arts, criminal justice, foundations and non-profit organizations, government, health care, and other human services.

Depending on the topic of interest, there are professional groups which look to the quality and rigor of the _____ process.

a. AMEX
b. AIG
c. ABC Television Network
d. Evaluation

6. The _____ is a private, not-for-profit organization whose primary purpose is to develop generally accepted accounting principles (GAAP) within the United States in the public's interest. The Securities and Exchange Commission (SEC) designated the _____ as the organization responsible for setting accounting standards for public companies in the U.S. It was created in 1973, replacing the Accounting Principles Board and the Committee on Accounting Procedure of the American Institute of Certified Public Accountants. The _____'s mission is 'to establish and improve standards of financial accounting and reporting for the guidance and education of the public, including issuers, auditors, and users of financial information.'

The _____ is not a governmental body.

a. Governmental Accounting Standards Board
b. Public company
c. Fannie Mae
d. Financial Accounting Standards Board

7. _____ is an umbrella term which refers to the various accounting systems used by various public sector entities. In the United States, for instance, there are two levels of government which follow different accounting standards set forth by independent, private sector boards. At the federal level, the Federal Accounting Standards Advisory Board (FASAB) sets forth the accounting standards to follow.

Chapter 2. The Logic of the Budget Process

a. Management accounting
b. Nonassurance services
c. Product control
d. Governmental accounting

8. Employment is a contract between two parties, one being the employer and the other being the _____. An _____ may be defined as: 'A person in the service of another under any contract of hire, express or implied, oral or written, where the employer has the power or right to control and direct the _____ in the material details of how the work is to be performed.' Black's Law Dictionary page 471 (5th ed. 1979.)
   a. AMEX
   b. ABC Television Network
   c. Employee
   d. AIG

9. _____ is any physical or virtual entity that is owned by an individual or jointly by a group of individuals. An owner of _____ has the right to consume, sell, rent, mortgage, transfer and exchange his or her _____. Important widely-recognized types of _____ include real _____, personal _____ (other physical possessions), and intellectual _____ (rights over artistic creations, inventions, etc.), although the latter is not always as widely recognized or enforced.
   a. Fiduciary
   b. Primary authority
   c. Disclosure requirement
   d. Property

10. _____ is a common concept in economics, and gives rise to derived concepts such as consumer debt. Generally _____ is defined by opposition to production. But the precise definition can vary because different schools of economists define production quite differently.
    a. Yield
    b. Consumption
    c. Mitigating Control
    d. Starving the beast

11. _____ is the term used to refer to the standard framework of guidelines for financial accounting used in any given jurisdiction. _____ includes the standards, conventions, and rules accountants follow in recording and summarizing transactions, and in the preparation of financial statements.

Financial accounting information must be assembled and reported objectively.

a. Current asset
b. Long-term liabilities
c. General ledger
d. Generally accepted accounting principles

12. In economics and sociology, an _____ is any factor (financial or non-financial) that enables or motivates a particular course of action, or counts as a reason for preferring one choice to the alternatives. It is an expectation that encourages people to behave in a certain way. Since human beings are purposeful creatures, the study of _____ structures is central to the study of all economic activity (both in terms of individual decision-making and in terms of co-operation and competition within a larger institutional structure.)
a. AMEX
b. Incentive
c. ABC Television Network
d. AIG

Chapter 3. Budget Structures and Institutions: Federal and State-Local

1. Project _____: The project _____ is a prediction of the costs associated with a particular company project. These costs include labor, materials, and other related expenses. The project _____ is often broken down into specific tasks, with task _____s assigned to each.
   a. 3M Company
   b. BNSF Railway
   c. BMC Software, Inc.
   d. Budget

2. In the United States, _____ federal benefits is defined as any federal program, project, service, and activity provided by the federal government that directly assists or benefits the American public in the areas of education, health, public safety, public welfare, and public works, among others. The assistance, which can reach to over $400 billion dollars annually, is provided and administered by federal government agencies, such as the U.S. Department of Housing and Urban Development and the U.S. Department of Health and Human Services, through special programs to recipients.

   The term assistance is defined by the federal government as:

   In order to provide _____ in an organized manner, the federal government provides assistance through federal agencies.

   a. Federal assistance
   b. BMC Software, Inc.
   c. BNSF Railway
   d. 3M Company

3. A budget _____ occurs when an entity spends more money than it takes in. The opposite of a budget _____ is a budget surplus. Debt is essentially an accumulated flow of _____s.
   a. Progressive tax
   b. Windfall profits tax
   c. Land value taxation
   d. Deficit

4. _____ is a common concept in economics, and gives rise to derived concepts such as consumer debt. Generally _____ is defined by opposition to production. But the precise definition can vary because different schools of economists define production quite differently.
   a. Starving the beast
   b. Yield
   c. Mitigating Control
   d. Consumption

5. A _____ refers to the process by which governments create and approve a budget. Â· The Financial Service Department prepares worksheets to assist the department head in preparation of department budget estimates Â· The Administrator calls a meeting of managers and they present and discuss plans for the following yeare;s projected level of activity. Â· The managers can work with the Financial Services, or work alone to prepare an estimate for the departments coming year.
   a. 3M Company
   b. Budget process
   c. BMC Software, Inc.
   d. BNSF Railway

6. The _____ is a federal agency within the legislative branch of the United States government. It is a government agency that provides economic data to Congress. It was created by the Congressional Budget and Impoundment Control Act of 1974.
   a. General Accounting Office
   b. 3M Company
   c. BMC Software, Inc.
   d. Congressional Budget Office

7. The _____ is a Cabinet-level office, and is the largest office within the Executive Office of the President of the United States (EOP.) It is an important conduit by which the White House oversees the activities of federal agencies. OMB is tasked with giving expert advice to senior White House officials on a range of topics relating to federal policy, management, legislative, regulatory, and budgetary issues.
   a. AT'T Wireless Services, Inc.
   b. Alaska Air Group
   c. Office of Management and Budget
   d. Analysis of variance

8. _____ is the act of taking possession of or assigning purpose to properties or ideas and is important in many topics, including:

   - _____ in relation to the spread of knowledge
   - _____ (art)
     - _____ (music) in reference to the re-use and proliferation of different types of music
   - _____ (economics) origination of human ownership of previously unowned natural resources such as land
   - _____ (law) as a component of government spending
   - Cultural _____ is the borrowing, or theft, of an element of cultural expression of one group by another.
   - The tort of _____ is one form of invasion of privacy.

Chapter 3. Budget Structures and Institutions: Federal and State-Local

a. Improvement
b. Appropriation
c. Intangible
d. Annuity

9. A _____ is a piece of paper, often preprinted in a way designed to help organize material for learning or clear understanding. Students in a school may have 'fill-in-the-blank' sheets of questions, diagrams or maps to help them with their exercises. Students will often use _____s to review what has been taught in class.
   a. 3M Company
   b. BMC Software, Inc.
   c. Value based pricing
   d. Worksheet

10. Employment is a contract between two parties, one being the employer and the other being the _____. An _____ may be defined as: 'A person in the service of another under any contract of hire, express or implied, oral or written, where the employer has the power or right to control and direct the _____ in the material details of how the work is to be performed.' Black's Law Dictionary page 471 (5th ed. 1979.)
    a. Employee
    b. AMEX
    c. ABC Television Network
    d. AIG

11. A _____ is a fungible, negotiable instrument representing financial value. they are broadly categorized into debt securities (such as banknotes, bonds and debentures), and equity securities; e.g., common stocks. The company or other entity issuing the _____ is called the issuer.
    a. Tracking stock
    b. 3M Company
    c. Security
    d. BMC Software, Inc.

12. _____ in the United States currently refers to the federal Old-Age, Survivors, and Disability Insurance (OASDI) program.

Chapter 3. Budget Structures and Institutions: Federal and State-Local

The original _____ Act and the current version of the Act, as amended encompass several social welfare and social insurance programs. The larger and better known programs are:

- Federal Old-Age, Survivors, and Disability Insurance
- Unemployment benefits
- Temporary Assistance for Needy Families
- Health Insurance for Aged and Disabled (Medicare)
- Grants to States for Medical Assistance Programs (Medicaid)
- State Children's Health Insurance Program (SCHIP)
- Supplemental Security Income (Social Securityl)

U.S. _____ is a social insurance program funded through dedicated payroll taxes called Federal Insurance Contributions Act (FICA.) Tax deposits are formally entrusted to Federal Old-Age and Survivors Insurance Trust Fund, or Federal Disability Insurance Trust Fund, Federal Hospital Insurance Trust Fund or the Federal Supplementary Medical Insurance Trust Fund.

a. Comparable
b. Price-to-sales ratio
c. Sale
d. Social Security

13. _____ is a system for businesses and individuals to pay installments of their expected tax liability on their income from employment, business, or investment for the current income year.

In Australia, _____ withholding arrangements replaced pay as you earn arrangements when the new tax system was introduced in July 2000. The new arrangements did not confine themselves to employment arrangements and also replaced the Prescribed Payments System and the Reportable Payments System.

a. Shrinkage
b. Yield
c. Residence trusts
d. Pay-as-you-go

14. The term _____ refers to government debt, expenditures and revenues, or to finance (particularly financial revenue) in general.

- _____ deficit is the budget deficit of federal or local government
- _____ policy is the discretionary spending of governments. Contrasts with monetary policy.
- _____ year and _____ quarter are reporting periods for firms and other agencies.

Chapter 3. Budget Structures and Institutions: Federal and State-Local

See also

- Procurator _____ and Crown Office and Procurator _____ Service

a. Comparable
b. Scientific Research and Experimental Development Tax Incentive Program
c. Swap
d. Fiscal

15. In economics, _____ or _____ goods or real _____ refers to factors of production used to create goods or services that are not themselves significantly consumed (though they may depreciate) in the production process. _____ goods may be acquired with money or financial _____. In finance and accounting, _____ generally refers to financial wealth, especially that used to start or maintain a business.
   a. Vyborg Appeal
   b. Capital
   c. Screening
   d. Disclosure

16. _____ is that which is owed; usually referencing assets owed, but the term can also cover moral obligations and other interactions not requiring money. In the case of assets, _____ is a means of using future purchasing power in the present before a summation has been earned. Some companies and corporations use _____ as a part of their overall corporate finance strategy.
   a. Debenture
   b. Debt
   c. Lender
   d. Loan

Chapter 4. Budget Methods and Practices

1. Project _____: The project _____ is a prediction of the costs associated with a particular company project. These costs include labor, materials, and other related expenses. The project _____ is often broken down into specific tasks, with task _____s assigned to each.
   a. 3M Company
   b. Budget
   c. BNSF Railway
   d. BMC Software, Inc.

2. In economics, _____ or _____ goods or real _____ refers to factors of production used to create goods or services that are not themselves significantly consumed (though they may depreciate) in the production process. _____ goods may be acquired with money or financial _____. In finance and accounting, _____ generally refers to financial wealth, especially that used to start or maintain a business.
   a. Vyborg Appeal
   b. Screening
   c. Capital
   d. Disclosure

3. _____ is the planning process used to determine whether a firm's long term investments such as new machinery, replacement machinery, new plants, new products, and research development projects are worth pursuing. It is budget for major capital, or investment, expenditures.

   Many formal methods are used in _____, including the techniques such as

   - Net present value
   - Profitability index
   - Internal rate of return
   - Modified Internal Rate of Return
   - Equivalent annuity

   These methods use the incremental cash flows from each potential investment, or project. Techniques based on accounting earnings and accounting rules are sometimes used - though economists consider this to be improper - such as the accounting rate of return, and 'return on investment.' Simplified and hybrid methods are used as well, such as payback period and discounted payback period.

   a. Capital budgeting
   b. Cash flow
   c. Gross profit
   d. Preferred stock

Chapter 4. Budget Methods and Practices 13

4. _____ is a common concept in economics, and gives rise to derived concepts such as consumer debt. Generally _____ is defined by opposition to production. But the precise definition can vary because different schools of economists define production quite differently.

   a. Mitigating Control
   b. Yield
   c. Starving the beast
   d. Consumption

5. In economics, business, retail, and accounting, a _____ is the value of money that has been used up to produce something, and hence is not available for use anymore. In economics, a _____ is an alternative that is given up as a result of a decision. In business, the _____ may be one of acquisition, in which case the amount of money expended to acquire it is counted as _____.

   a. Cost of quality
   b. Prime cost
   c. Cost
   d. Cost allocation

6. _____ is an area of engineering practice concerned with the 'application of scientific principles and techniques to problems of cost estimating, cost control, business planning and management science, profitability analysis, project management, and planning and scheduling.'

Key objectives of _____ are to arrive at accurate cost estimates and to avoid cost overruns. The broad array of _____ topics represent the intersection of the fields of project management, business management, and engineering. Most people have a limited view of what engineering encompasses.

   a. 3M Company
   b. BMC Software, Inc.
   c. Cost engineering
   d. BNSF Railway

7. _____ is the calculated approximation of a result which is usable even if input data may be incomplete or uncertain.

In statistics, see _____ theory, estimator.

In mathematics, approximation or _____ typically means finding upper or lower bounds of a quantity that cannot readily be computed precisely and is also an educated guess .

a. ABC Television Network
b. AIG
c. AMEX
d. Estimation

8. _____ is that which is owed; usually referencing assets owed, but the term can also cover moral obligations and other interactions not requiring money. In the case of assets, _____ is a means of using future purchasing power in the present before a summation has been earned. Some companies and corporations use _____ as a part of their overall corporate finance strategy.
   a. Debt
   b. Debenture
   c. Loan
   d. Lender

9. A _____ is a piece of paper, often preprinted in a way designed to help organize material for learning or clear understanding. Students in a school may have 'fill-in-the-blank' sheets of questions, diagrams or maps to help them with their exercises. Students will often use _____s to review what has been taught in class.
   a. BMC Software, Inc.
   b. 3M Company
   c. Worksheet
   d. Value based pricing

10. _____, in general, is the investigation of a great number of something (for instance, people) looking for those with a particular problem or feature. One example is at an airport, where many bags get x-rayed to try to detect any which may contain weapons or explosives. People are also screened going through a metal detector.
    a. Pay-as-you-go
    b. Screening
    c. Capital
    d. General partner

11. One of the reforms of the Progressive Era in the United States was the _____ system which had its first application for municipal government. The federal government conducted an important study of the _____ system during the administration of President William Howard Taft (See Sec. VI: The Taft Commission's Federal Budget Study, pp.

a. AMEX
b. Executive budget
c. ABC Television Network
d. AIG

12. A budget _____ occurs when an entity spends more money than it takes in. The opposite of a budget _____ is a budget surplus. Debt is essentially an accumulated flow of _____s.
   a. Land value taxation
   b. Progressive tax
   c. Windfall profits tax
   d. Deficit

13. A _____ is a charge for the use of a product or service.

A _____ may apply per use of the good or service or charge the user for use of the good or service. The first is a charge for each time while the second is a charge for bulk or time-limited use.

   a. Optimal tax
   b. Indirect tax
   c. Association of Real Estate Taxpayers
   d. User charge

14. An _____ is a term used in behavioral economics to describe those types of behaviors that impose costs on a person in the long-run that are not taken into account when making decisions in the present. Classical Economics discourages government from creating legislation that targets internalities, because it is assumed that the consumer takes these personal costs into account when paying for the good that causes the _____. For example, cigarettes should be taxed because of the negative consumption externalities that they impose, such as second-hand smoke, not because the smoker harms him or herself by smoking.
   a. Internality
   b. Inventory turnover ratio
   c. Authorised capital
   d. Operating budget

15. In accounting and organizational theory, _____ is defined as a process effected by an organization's structure, work and authority flows, people and management information systems, designed to help the organization accomplish specific goals or objectives. It is a means by which an organization's resources are directed, monitored, and measured. It plays an important role in preventing and detecting fraud and protecting the organization's resources, both physical (e.g., machinery and property) and intangible (e.g., reputation or intellectual property such as trademarks.)

a. Audit risk
b. Auditor independence
c. Audit committee
d. Internal control

16. The general definition of an _____ is an evaluation of a person, organization, system, process, project or product. _____s are performed to ascertain the validity and reliability of information; also to provide an assessment of a system's internal control. The goal of an _____ is to express an opinion on the person/organization/system (etc) in question, under evaluation based on work done on a test basis.
   a. Assurance service
   b. Institute of Chartered Accountants of India
   c. Audit regime
   d. Audit

17. _____ is systematic determination of merit, worth, and significance of something or someone using criteria against a set of standards. _____ often is used to characterize and appraise subjects of interest in a wide range of human enterprises, including the arts, criminal justice, foundations and non-profit organizations, government, health care, and other human services.

Depending on the topic of interest, there are professional groups which look to the quality and rigor of the _____ process.

   a. AIG
   b. Evaluation
   c. ABC Television Network
   d. AMEX

Chapter 5. Budget Classifications and Reform

1. Project _____: The project _____ is a prediction of the costs associated with a particular company project. These costs include labor, materials, and other related expenses. The project _____ is often broken down into specific tasks, with task _____s assigned to each.
   a. BMC Software, Inc.
   b. 3M Company
   c. BNSF Railway
   d. Budget

2. _____ is one of the four Ps of the marketing mix. The other three aspects are product, promotion, and place. It is also a key variable in microeconomic price allocation theory.
   a. Pricing
   b. Cost-plus pricing
   c. Target costing
   d. Price

3. In economics, _____ or _____ goods or real _____ refers to factors of production used to create goods or services that are not themselves significantly consumed (though they may depreciate) in the production process. _____ goods may be acquired with money or financial _____. In finance and accounting, _____ generally refers to financial wealth, especially that used to start or maintain a business.
   a. Vyborg Appeal
   b. Disclosure
   c. Screening
   d. Capital

4. _____ is a costing model that identifies activities in an organization and assigns the cost of each activity resource to all products and services according to the actual consumption by each: it assigns more indirect costs (overhead) into direct costs.

In this way an organization can establish the true cost of its individual products and services for the purposes of identifying and eliminating those which are unprofitable and lowering the prices of those which are overpriced.

In a business organization, the ABC methodology assigns an organization's resource costs through activities to the products and services provided to its customers.

   a. Indirect costs
   b. ABC Television Network
   c. Activity-based management
   d. Activity-based costing

Chapter 5. Budget Classifications and Reform

5. A _____ is a legal document that is often passed by the legislature, and approved by the chief executive-or president. For example, only certain types of revenue may be imposed and collected. Property tax is frequently the basis for municipal and county revenues, while sales tax and/or income tax are the basis for state revenues, and income tax and corporate tax are the basis for national revenues.
   a. 3M Company
   b. Value capture
   c. BMC Software, Inc.
   d. Government Budget

6. _____ consists of the sale of goods or merchandise from a fixed location, such as a department store, boutique or kiosk in small or individual lots for direct consumption by the purchaser. _____ may include subordinated services, such as delivery. Purchasers may be individuals or businesses.
   a. BNSF Railway
   b. Retailing
   c. 3M Company
   d. BMC Software, Inc.

7. A _____ is the pinnacle activity involved in selling products or services in return for money or other compensation. It is an act of completion of a commercial activity.

A _____ is completed by the seller, the owner of the goods.

   a. Maturity
   b. High yield stock
   c. Tertiary sector of economy
   d. Sale

8. _____ is any physical or virtual entity that is owned by an individual or jointly by a group of individuals. An owner of _____ has the right to consume, sell, rent, mortgage, transfer and exchange his or her _____. Important widely-recognized types of _____ include real _____, personal _____ (other physical possessions), and intellectual _____ (rights over artistic creations, inventions, etc.), although the latter is not always as widely recognized or enforced.
   a. Disclosure requirement
   b. Primary authority
   c. Fiduciary
   d. Property

Chapter 5. Budget Classifications and Reform

9. _____ or net present worth (NPW) is defined as the total present value (PV) of a time series of cash flows. It is a standard method for using the time value of money to appraise long-term projects. Used for capital budgeting, and widely throughout economics, it measures the excess or shortfall of cash flows, in present value terms, once financing charges are met.

   a. Present value
   b. Future value
   c. 3M Company
   d. Net present value

10. _____ is the value on a given date of a future payment or series of future payments, discounted to reflect the time value of money and other factors such as investment risk. _____ calculations are widely used in business and economics to provide a means to compare cash flows at different times on a meaningful 'like to like' basis.

The most commonly applied model of the time value of money is compound interest.

   a. 3M Company
   b. Future value
   c. Net present value
   d. Present value

11. _____ is the act of taking possession of or assigning purpose to properties or ideas and is important in many topics, including:

   - _____ in relation to the spread of knowledge
   - _____ (art)
     - _____ (music) in reference to the re-use and proliferation of different types of music
   - _____ (economics) origination of human ownership of previously unowned natural resources such as land
   - _____ (law) as a component of government spending
   - Cultural _____ is the borrowing, or theft, of an element of cultural expression of one group by another.
   - The tort of _____ is one form of invasion of privacy.

   a. Annuity
   b. Improvement
   c. Intangible
   d. Appropriation

12. _____ is a process of agreeing upon objectives within an organization so that management and employees agree to the objectives and understand what they are in the organization.

Chapter 5. Budget Classifications and Reform

The term '_____' was first popularized by Peter Drucker in his 1954 book 'The Practice of Management'.

The essence of _____ is participative goal setting, choosing course of actions and decision making.

a. Management by objectives
b. Best practice
c. Trustee
d. Cash cow

13. The _____ is a Cabinet-level office, and is the largest office within the Executive Office of the President of the United States (EOP.) It is an important conduit by which the White House oversees the activities of federal agencies. OMB is tasked with giving expert advice to senior White House officials on a range of topics relating to federal policy, management, legislative, regulatory, and budgetary issues.
a. Analysis of variance
b. AT'T Wireless Services, Inc.
c. Alaska Air Group
d. Office of Management and Budget

Chapter 6. Capital Budgeting, Public Infrastructure Investment, and Project Evaluation

1. Project _____: The project _____ is a prediction of the costs associated with a particular company project. These costs include labor, materials, and other related expenses. The project _____ is often broken down into specific tasks, with task _____s assigned to each.
   a. BMC Software, Inc.
   b. BNSF Railway
   c. Budget
   d. 3M Company

2. In economics, _____ or _____ goods or real _____ refers to factors of production used to create goods or services that are not themselves significantly consumed (though they may depreciate) in the production process. _____ goods may be acquired with money or financial _____. In finance and accounting, _____ generally refers to financial wealth, especially that used to start or maintain a business.
   a. Disclosure
   b. Screening
   c. Vyborg Appeal
   d. Capital

3. _____ is the planning process used to determine whether a firm's long term investments such as new machinery, replacement machinery, new plants, new products, and research development projects are worth pursuing. It is budget for major capital, or investment, expenditures.

Many formal methods are used in _____, including the techniques such as

- Net present value
- Profitability index
- Internal rate of return
- Modified Internal Rate of Return
- Equivalent annuity

These methods use the incremental cash flows from each potential investment, or project. Techniques based on accounting earnings and accounting rules are sometimes used - though economists consider this to be improper - such as the accounting rate of return, and 'return on investment.' Simplified and hybrid methods are used as well, such as payback period and discounted payback period.

   a. Gross profit
   b. Cash flow
   c. Preferred stock
   d. Capital budgeting

22   *Chapter 6. Capital Budgeting, Public Infrastructure Investment, and Project Evaluation*

4. The _____ is a federal agency within the legislative branch of the United States government. It is a government agency that provides economic data to Congress. It was created by the Congressional Budget and Impoundment Control Act of 1974.

   a. 3M Company
   b. Congressional Budget Office
   c. General Accounting Office
   d. BMC Software, Inc.

5. _____ is systematic determination of merit, worth, and significance of something or someone using criteria against a set of standards. _____ often is used to characterize and appraise subjects of interest in a wide range of human enterprises, including the arts, criminal justice, foundations and non-profit organizations, government, health care, and other human services.

Depending on the topic of interest, there are professional groups which look to the quality and rigor of the _____ process.

   a. AMEX
   b. AIG
   c. ABC Television Network
   d. Evaluation

6. _____ is the act of taking possession of or assigning purpose to properties or ideas and is important in many topics, including:

   - _____ in relation to the spread of knowledge
   - _____ (art)
     - _____ (music) in reference to the re-use and proliferation of different types of music
   - _____ (economics) origination of human ownership of previously unowned natural resources such as land
   - _____ (law) as a component of government spending
   - Cultural _____ is the borrowing, or theft, of an element of cultural expression of one group by another.
   - The tort of _____ is one form of invasion of privacy.

   a. Intangible
   b. Annuity
   c. Appropriation
   d. Improvement

Chapter 6. Capital Budgeting, Public Infrastructure Investment, and Project Evaluation

7. The general definition of an _____ is an evaluation of a person, organization, system, process, project or product. _____s are performed to ascertain the validity and reliability of information; also to provide an assessment of a system's internal control. The goal of an _____ is to express an opinion on the person/organization/system (etc) in question, under evaluation based on work done on a test basis.
    a. Audit
    b. Institute of Chartered Accountants of India
    c. Assurance service
    d. Audit regime

8. A _____ is a piece of paper, often preprinted in a way designed to help organize material for learning or clear understanding. Students in a school may have 'fill-in-the-blank' sheets of questions, diagrams or maps to help them with their exercises. Students will often use _____s to review what has been taught in class.
    a. BMC Software, Inc.
    b. Value based pricing
    c. Worksheet
    d. 3M Company

9. The term _____ has three unrelated technical definitions, and is also used in a variety of non-technical ways.

    - In financial economics, it refers to any asset used to make money, as opposed to assets used for personal enjoyment or consumption. This is an important distinction because two people can disagree sharply about the value of personal assets, one person might think a sports car is more valuable than a pickup truck, another person might have the opposite taste. But if an asset is held for the purpose of making money, taste has nothing to do with it, only differences of opinion about how much money the asset will produce. With the further assumption that people agree on the probability distribution of future cash flows, it is possible to have an objective _____ pricing model. Even without the assumption of agreement, it is possible to set rational limits on _____ value.
    - In governmental accounting, it is defined as any asset used in operations with an initial useful life extending beyond one reporting period. Generally, government managers have a 'stewardship' duty to maintain _____s under their control. See International Public Sector Accounting Standards for details.
    - In US tax accounting, it is defined as any property other than a list of exceptions. The main exceptions are anything held for sale, and any real estate or depreciable property used in business. Almost everything you own and use for personal purposes, pleasure or investment is a _____. If something is a _____ for tax purposes, gains or losses on sale or disposition are capital gains or capital losses. For individuals, however, capital losses on property held for personal use are generally not deductible. See the IRS publication Tax Facts about Capital Gains and Losses for details.

A well-known financial accounting textbook advises that the term be avoided except in tax accounting because it is used in so many different senses, not all of them well-defined. For example it is often used as a synonym for fixed assets or for investments in securities.

A common non-technical usage occurs when people ask that employees or the environment or something else be treated as a _____.

Chapter 6. Capital Budgeting, Public Infrastructure Investment, and Project Evaluation

a. Solvency
b. 3M Company
c. BMC Software, Inc.
d. Capital asset

10. In business and accounting, _____ are everything of value that is owned by a person or company. It is a claim on the property your income of a borrower. The balance sheet of a firm records the monetary value of the _____ owned by the firm.
   a. Accounts receivable
   b. Earnings before interest, taxes, depreciation and amortization
   c. Accrual basis accounting
   d. Assets

11. In probability theory and statistics, the index of dispersion, dispersion index, _____ like the coefficient of variation, is a normalized measure of the dispersion of a probability distribution: it is a measure used to quantify whether a set of observed occurrences are relatively clustered or dispersed compared to a standard statistical model.

It is defined as the ratio of the variance $>\sigma^2$ to the mean $>\mu$,

It is also known as the Fano factor, though this latter is sometimes reserved for windowed data (the mean and variance are computed over a subpopulation), where the index of dispersion is the special case where the window is infinite. Windowing data is frequently done: the VMR is frequently computed over various intervals in time or small regions in space, which may be called 'windows', and the resulting statistic called the Fano factor.

   a. BNSF Railway
   b. Coefficient of dispersion
   c. 3M Company
   d. BMC Software, Inc.

12. _____ is the realization of an application idea, model, design, specification, standard, algorithm an _____ is a realization of a technical specification or algorithm as a program, software component, or other computer system. Many _____ s may exist for a given specification or standard.

Chapter 6. Capital Budgeting, Public Infrastructure Investment, and Project Evaluation

a. ABC Television Network
b. AMEX
c. AIG
d. Implementation

13. _____ is a financial mechanism in which a debtor obtains the right to delay payments to a creditor, for a defined period of time, in exchange for a charge or fee. Essentially, the party that owes money in the present purchases the right to delay the payment until some future date. The discount, or charge, is simply the difference between the original amount owed in the present and the amount that has to be paid in the future to settle the debt.

a. Discounting
b. Risk aversion
c. Discount factor
d. Risk adjusted return on capital

14. _____ is a term that refers both to:

- a formal discipline used to help appraise, or assess, the case for a project or proposal, which itself is a process known as project appraisal; and
- an informal approach to making decisions of any kind.

Under both definitions the process involves, whether explicitly or implicitly, weighing the total expected costs against the total expected benefits of one or more actions in order to choose the best or most profitable option. The formal process is often referred to as either CBA (_____) or BCost-benefit analysis

A hallmark of CBA is that all benefits and all costs are expressed in money terms, and are adjusted for the time value of money, so that all flows of benefits and flows of project costs over time (which tend to occur at different points in time) are expressed on a common basis in terms of their 'e;present value.'e; Closely related, but slightly different, formal techniques include Cost-effectiveness analysis, Economic impact analysis, Fiscal impact analysis and Social Return on Investment(SROI) analysis. The latter builds upon the logic of _____, but differs in that it is explicitly designed to inform the practical decision-making of enterprise managers and investors focused on optimising their social and environmental impacts.

a. BNSF Railway
b. 3M Company
c. BMC Software, Inc.
d. Cost-benefit analysis

15. _____ is the calculated approximation of a result which is usable even if input data may be incomplete or uncertain.

Chapter 6. Capital Budgeting, Public Infrastructure Investment, and Project Evaluation

In statistics, see _____ theory, estimator.

In mathematics, approximation or _____ typically means finding upper or lower bounds of a quantity that cannot readily be computed precisely and is also an educated guess .

a. Estimation
b. ABC Television Network
c. AMEX
d. AIG

16. In economics, business, retail, and accounting, a _____ is the value of money that has been used up to produce something, and hence is not available for use anymore. In economics, a _____ is an alternative that is given up as a result of a decision. In business, the _____ may be one of acquisition, in which case the amount of money expended to acquire it is counted as _____.
a. Cost of quality
b. Cost
c. Prime cost
d. Cost allocation

17. Discounting is a financial mechanism in which a debtor obtains the right to delay payments to a creditor, for a defined period of time, in exchange for a charge or fee. Essentially, the party that owes money in the present purchases the right to delay the payment until some future date. The _____, or charge, is simply the difference between the original amount owed in the present and the amount that has to be paid in the future to settle the debt.
a. Discount
b. Discount factor
c. Risk aversion
d. Discounting

18. The _____ is an interest rate a central bank charges depository institutions that borrow reserves from it.

Chapter 6. Capital Budgeting, Public Infrastructure Investment, and Project Evaluation

The term _____ has two meanings:

- the same as interest rate; the term 'discount' does not refer to the meaning of the word, but to the purpose of using the quantity, such as computations of present value, e.g. net present value or discounted cash flow

- the annual effective _____, which is the annual interest divided by the capital including that interest; this rate is lower than the interest rate; it corresponds to using the value after a year as the nominal value, and seeing the initial value as the nominal value minus a discount; it is used for Treasury Bills and similar financial instruments

The annual effective _____ is the annual interest divided by the capital including that interest, which is the interest rate divided by 100% plus the interest rate. It is the annual discount factor to be applied to the future cash flow, to find the discount, subtracted from a future value to find the value one year earlier.

For example, suppose there is a government bond that sells for $95 and pays $100 in a year's time.

a. Process time
b. Municipal bond
c. Convertible bond
d. Discount rate

Chapter 7. Taxation: Criteria for Evaluating Revenue Options

1. In finance, an _____ is a contract between a buyer and a seller that gives the buyer the right--but not the obligation-- to buy or to sell a particular asset (the underlying asset) at a later time at an agreed price. In return for granting the _____, the seller collects a payment (the premium) from the buyer. A call _____ gives the buyer the right to buy the underlying asset; a put _____ gives the buyer of the _____ the right to sell the underlying asset.

   a. ABC Television Network
   b. AIG
   c. AMEX
   d. Option

2. _____ is that which is owed; usually referencing assets owed, but the term can also cover moral obligations and other interactions not requiring money. In the case of assets, _____ is a means of using future purchasing power in the present before a summation has been earned. Some companies and corporations use _____ as a part of their overall corporate finance strategy.

   a. Debenture
   b. Debt
   c. Lender
   d. Loan

3. _____ is a common concept in economics, and gives rise to derived concepts such as consumer debt. Generally _____ is defined by opposition to production. But the precise definition can vary because different schools of economists define production quite differently.

   a. Starving the beast
   b. Mitigating Control
   c. Consumption
   d. Yield

4. A municipality is an administrative entity composed of a clearly defined territory and its population and commonly denotes a city, town or a small grouping of them. A municipality is typically governed by a mayor and a city council or _____ council.

   The notion of municipality includes townships but is not restricted to them.

   a. 3M Company
   b. BMC Software, Inc.
   c. BNSF Railway
   d. Municipal

Chapter 7. Taxation: Criteria for Evaluating Revenue Options

5. In finance, the term _____ describes the amount in cash that returns to the owners of a security. Normally it does not include the price variations, at the difference of the total return. _____ applies to various stated rates of return on stocks (common and preferred, and convertible), fixed income instruments (bonds, notes, bills, strips, zero coupon), and some other investment type insurance products (e.g. annuities.)
   a. Residence trusts
   b. Disclosure
   c. Pension System
   d. Yield

6. In probability theory and statistics, the index of dispersion, dispersion index, _____ like the coefficient of variation, is a normalized measure of the dispersion of a probability distribution: it is a measure used to quantify whether a set of observed occurrences are relatively clustered or dispersed compared to a standard statistical model.

It is defined as the ratio of the variance $>\sigma^2$ to the mean $>\mu$,

It is also known as the Fano factor, though this latter is sometimes reserved for windowed data (the mean and variance are computed over a subpopulation), where the index of dispersion is the special case where the window is infinite. Windowing data is frequently done: the VMR is frequently computed over various intervals in time or small regions in space, which may be called 'windows', and the resulting statistic called the Fano factor.

   a. 3M Company
   b. BNSF Railway
   c. BMC Software, Inc.
   d. Coefficient of dispersion

7. An _____ is a tax levied on the financial income of people, corporations, or other legal entities. Various _____ systems exist, with varying degrees of tax incidence. Income taxation can be progressive, proportional, or regressive.
   a. Individual Retirement Arrangement
   b. Income Tax
   c. Implied level of government service
   d. Ordinary income

8. A _____ is the transfer of wealth from one party (such as a person or company) to another. A _____ is usually made in exchange for the provision of goods, services or both, or to fulfill a legal obligation.

The simplest and oldest form of _____ is barter, the exchange of one good or service for another.

Chapter 7. Taxation: Criteria for Evaluating Revenue Options

   a. 3M Company
   b. BMC Software, Inc.
   c. Payment
   d. Payee

9. _____ is any physical or virtual entity that is owned by an individual or jointly by a group of individuals. An owner of _____ has the right to consume, sell, rent, mortgage, transfer and exchange his or her _____. Important widely-recognized types of _____ include real _____, personal _____ (other physical possessions), and intellectual _____ (rights over artistic creations, inventions, etc.), although the latter is not always as widely recognized or enforced.
   a. Disclosure requirement
   b. Property
   c. Fiduciary
   d. Primary authority

10. A _____ is a fungible, negotiable instrument representing financial value. they are broadly categorized into debt securities (such as banknotes, bonds and debentures), and equity securities; e.g., common stocks. The company or other entity issuing the _____ is called the issuer.
   a. BMC Software, Inc.
   b. Tracking stock
   c. 3M Company
   d. Security

11. The term _____ describes two different concepts:

   - The first is a recognition of partial payment already made towards taxes due.
   - The second is a state benefit paid to workers through the tax system, which has the effect of increasing (rather than reducing) net income.

Within the Australian, Canadian, United Kingdom, and United States tax systems, a _____ is a recognition of partial payment already made towards taxes due. A similar concept exists (fr:Avoir fiscal) in the French tax system. This situation arises, for example, when standard rate tax has been deducted at source , but the tax-payer is subject to further taxation at a higher rate. It also applies in dividend imputation systems.

   a. 3M Company
   b. Foreign tax credit
   c. Tax credit
   d. Scientific Research and Experimental Development Tax Incentive Program

Chapter 7. Taxation: Criteria for Evaluating Revenue Options

12. _____ , is a 'supply-side' economist who became influential during the Reagan administration as a member of Reagan's Economic Policy Advisory Board (1981-1989.)

Laffer is best known for the Laffer curve, a curve illustrating tax elasticity which asserts that in certain situations, a decrease in tax rates could result in an increase in tax revenues. Although he does not claim to have invented this concept (Laffer, 2004), it was popularized with policy-makers following an afternoon meeting with Dick Cheney and Donald Rumsfeld in which he reportedly sketched the curve on a napkin to illustrate his argument (Wanniski, 2005.)

   a. Alan Greenspan
   b. Abby Joseph Cohen
   c. Boeing
   d. Arthur Betz Laffer

13. In economics, an _____ or spillover of an economic transaction is an impact on a party that is not directly involved in the transaction. In such a case, prices do not reflect the full costs or benefits in production or consumption of a product or service. A positive impact is called an external benefit, while a negative impact is called an external cost.
   a. AIG
   b. ABC Television Network
   c. AMEX
   d. Externality

Chapter 8. Major Tax Structures: Income Taxes

1. An _____ is a tax levied on the financial income of people, corporations, or other legal entities. Various _____ systems exist, with varying degrees of tax incidence. Income taxation can be progressive, proportional, or regressive.
   a. Income tax
   b. Implied level of government service
   c. Individual Retirement Arrangement
   d. Ordinary income

2. In economics, an _____ or spillover of an economic transaction is an impact on a party that is not directly involved in the transaction. In such a case, prices do not reflect the full costs or benefits in production or consumption of a product or service. A positive impact is called an external benefit, while a negative impact is called an external cost.
   a. AIG
   b. AMEX
   c. ABC Television Network
   d. Externality

3. _____ is any physical or virtual entity that is owned by an individual or jointly by a group of individuals. An owner of _____ has the right to consume, sell, rent, mortgage, transfer and exchange his or her _____. Important widely-recognized types of _____ include real _____, personal _____ (other physical possessions), and intellectual _____ (rights over artistic creations, inventions, etc.), although the latter is not always as widely recognized or enforced.
   a. Fiduciary
   b. Primary authority
   c. Property
   d. Disclosure requirement

4. The United States federal _____ is a refundable tax credit. For tax year 2008, a claimant with one qualifying child can receive a maximum credit of $2,917. For two or more qualifying children, the maximum credit is $4,824.
   a. Uniform Gifts to Minors Act
   b. IRS penalties
   c. Ordinary income
   d. Earned income tax credit

5. In probability theory and statistics, the index of dispersion, dispersion index, _____ like the coefficient of variation, is a normalized measure of the dispersion of a probability distribution: it is a measure used to quantify whether a set of observed occurrences are relatively clustered or dispersed compared to a standard statistical model.

Chapter 8. Major Tax Structures: Income Taxes 33

It is defined as the ratio of the variance $>\sigma^2$ to the mean $>\mu$,

$$>$$

It is also known as the Fano factor, though this latter is sometimes reserved for windowed data (the mean and variance are computed over a subpopulation), where the index of dispersion is the special case where the window is infinite. Windowing data is frequently done: the VMR is frequently computed over various intervals in time or small regions in space, which may be called 'windows', and the resulting statistic called the Fano factor.

a. BMC Software, Inc.
b. 3M Company
c. BNSF Railway
d. Coefficient of Dispersion

6. The term _____ describes two different concepts:

- The first is a recognition of partial payment already made towards taxes due.
- The second is a state benefit paid to workers through the tax system, which has the effect of increasing (rather than reducing) net income.

Within the Australian, Canadian, United Kingdom, and United States tax systems, a _____ is a recognition of partial payment already made towards taxes due. A similar concept exists (fr:Avoir fiscal) in the French tax system. This situation arises, for example, when standard rate tax has been deducted at source , but the tax-payer is subject to further taxation at a higher rate. It also applies in dividend imputation systems.

a. Scientific Research and Experimental Development Tax Incentive Program
b. 3M Company
c. Foreign tax credit
d. Tax credit

7. _____ is commonly defined as the amount of a company's or a person's income before all deductions or any taxpayer's income, except that which is specifically excluded by the Internal Revenue Code, before taking deductions or taxes into account. For a business, this amount is pre-tax net sales less cost of sales. Section 61 of the Internal Revenue Code (Code) defines '_____' as 'all income from whatever source derived.' Section 61(a) of the Code lists fifteen examples of items included in _____; however, the list is not exhaustive.

Chapter 8. Major Tax Structures: Income Taxes

a. Gross income
b. Gross profit
c. Preferred stock
d. Gross profit margin

8. A _____ is a fungible, negotiable instrument representing financial value. they are broadly categorized into debt securities (such as banknotes, bonds and debentures), and equity securities; e.g., common stocks. The company or other entity issuing the _____ is called the issuer.
   a. BMC Software, Inc.
   b. Tracking stock
   c. 3M Company
   d. Security

9. Project _____: The project _____ is a prediction of the costs associated with a particular company project. These costs include labor, materials, and other related expenses. The project _____ is often broken down into specific tasks, with task _____s assigned to each.
   a. BMC Software, Inc.
   b. 3M Company
   c. BNSF Railway
   d. Budget

10. The _____ is a federal agency within the legislative branch of the United States government. It is a government agency that provides economic data to Congress. It was created by the Congressional Budget and Impoundment Control Act of 1974.
    a. BMC Software, Inc.
    b. 3M Company
    c. General Accounting Office
    d. Congressional Budget Office

11. A _____ is an exemption from all or certain taxes of a state or nation in which part of the taxes that would normally be collected from an individual or an organization are instead foregone.

Normally a _____ is provided to an individual or organization which falls within a class which the government wishes to promote economically, such as charitable organizations. _____s are usually meant to either reduce the tax burden on a particular segment of society in the interests of fairness or to promote some type of economic activity through reducing the tax burden on those organizations or individuals who are involved in that activity.

Chapter 8. Major Tax Structures: Income Taxes   35

a. Securities Turnover Excise Tax
b. Form W-4
c. Direct tax
d. Tax exemption

12. A _____ is the transfer of wealth from one party (such as a person or company) to another. A _____ is usually made in exchange for the provision of goods, services or both, or to fulfill a legal obligation.

The simplest and oldest form of _____ is barter, the exchange of one good or service for another.

a. BMC Software, Inc.
b. Payee
c. 3M Company
d. Payment

13. _____ is the portion of income that is the subject of taxation according to the laws that determine what is income and the taxation rate for that income. Generally, _____ refers to an individual's (or corporation's) gross income, adjusted for various deductions allowable by statute. The main questions put by most individuals in any jurisdiction are 'what makes up my _____' and what tax rates should be applied such that I can work out my tax liability to the state.

a. Half-year convention
b. SUTA dumping
c. Reverse Morris trust
d. Taxable income

14. _____ are the income that is gained by governments because of taxation of the people.

Just as there are different types of tax, the form in which _____ is collected also differs; furthermore, the agency that collects the tax may not be part of central government, but may be an alternative third-party licenced to collect tax which they themselves will use. For example:

- In the UK, the DVLA collects road tax, which is then passed on the treasury.

_____s on purchases can come from two forms: 'tax' itself is a percentage of the price added to the purchase (such as sales tax in US states, or VAT in the UK), while 'duty' is a fixed amount added to the purchase price (such as is commonly found on cigarettes.) In order to calculate the total tax raised from these sales, we must work out the effective tax rate multiplied by the quantity supplied.

a. Tax revenue
b. Life insurance tax shelter
c. National War Tax Resistance Coordinating Committee
d. Disposable income

15. _____ is a common concept in economics, and gives rise to derived concepts such as consumer debt. Generally _____ is defined by opposition to production. But the precise definition can vary because different schools of economists define production quite differently.
   a. Mitigating Control
   b. Starving the beast
   c. Yield
   d. Consumption

16. _____ is a technique to adjust income payments by means of a price index, in order to maintain the purchasing power of the public after inflation.

Applying a cost-of-living escalation COLA clause to a stream of periodic payments protects the real value of those payments and effectively transfers the risk of inflation from the payee to the payor, who must pay more each year to reflect the increases in prices. Thus, inflation _____ is often applied to pension payments, rents and other situations which are not subject to regular re-pricing in the market.

   a. AIG
   b. ABC Television Network
   c. Indexation
   d. AMEX

17. A _____ is any one of a variety of different systems, institutions, procedures, social relations and infrastructures whereby persons trade, and goods and services are exchanged, forming part of the economy. It is an arrangement that allows buyers and sellers to exchange things. _____s vary in size, range, geographic scale, location, types and variety of human communities, as well as the types of goods and services traded.
   a. Recession
   b. Perfect competition
   c. Market
   d. Market Failure

18. _____ is a specific term used in companies' financial reporting from the company-whole point of view. Because that use excludes the effects of changing ownership interest, an economic measure of _____ is necessary for financial analysis from the shareholders' point of view

Chapter 8. Major Tax Structures: Income Taxes

_____ is defined by the Financial Accounting Standards Board, or FASB, as 'the change in equity [net assets] of a business enterprise during a period from transactions and other events and circumstances from nonowner sources. It includes all changes in equity during a period except those resulting from investments by owners and distributions to owners.'

_____ is the sum of net income and other items that must bypass the income statement because they have not been realized, including items like an unrealized holding gain or loss from available for sale securities and foreign currency translation gains or losses.

a. 3M Company
b. BNSF Railway
c. Comprehensive income
d. BMC Software, Inc.

19. _____ is that which is owed; usually referencing assets owed, but the term can also cover moral obligations and other interactions not requiring money. In the case of assets, _____ is a means of using future purchasing power in the present before a summation has been earned. Some companies and corporations use _____ as a part of their overall corporate finance strategy.
a. Debenture
b. Debt
c. Lender
d. Loan

20. A municipality is an administrative entity composed of a clearly defined territory and its population and commonly denotes a city, town or a small grouping of them. A municipality is typically governed by a mayor and a city council or _____ council.

The notion of municipality includes townships but is not restricted to them.

a. 3M Company
b. Municipal
c. BMC Software, Inc.
d. BNSF Railway

21. In finance, the term _____ describes the amount in cash that returns to the owners of a security. Normally it does not include the price variations, at the difference of the total return. _____ applies to various stated rates of return on stocks (common and preferred, and convertible), fixed income instruments (bonds, notes, bills, strips, zero coupon), and some other investment type insurance products (e.g. annuities.)

Chapter 8. Major Tax Structures: Income Taxes

   a. Yield
   b. Pension System
   c. Disclosure
   d. Residence trusts

22. An _____ is a term used in behavioral economics to describe those types of behaviors that impose costs on a person in the long-run that are not taken into account when making decisions in the present. Classical Economics discourages government from creating legislation that targets internalities, because it is assumed that the consumer takes these personal costs into account when paying for the good that causes the _____. For example, cigarettes should be taxed because of the negative consumption externalities that they impose, such as second-hand smoke, not because the smoker harms him or herself by smoking.
   a. Internality
   b. Operating budget
   c. Authorised capital
   d. Inventory turnover ratio

23. The _____ is the United States federal government agency that collects taxes and enforces the internal revenue laws. It is an agency within the U.S. Dept of the treasury responsible for interpretation and application of Federal tax law. The official U.S. Treasury regulations provide (in part):

The _____ is a bureau of the Department of the Treasury under the immediate direction of the Commissioner of Internal Revenue.

   a. Use tax
   b. Income tax
   c. Indirect tax
   d. Internal Revenue Service

24. The general definition of an _____ is an evaluation of a person, organization, system, process, project or product. _____s are performed to ascertain the validity and reliability of information; also to provide an assessment of a system's internal control. The goal of an _____ is to express an opinion on the person/organization/system (etc) in question, under evaluation based on work done on a test basis.
   a. Assurance service
   b. Audit
   c. Institute of Chartered Accountants of India
   d. Audit regime

Chapter 8. Major Tax Structures: Income Taxes

25. In a company, _____ is the sum of all financial records of salaries, wages, bonuses and deductions.

A paycheck, is traditionally a paper document issued by an employer to pay an employee for services rendered. While most commonly used in the United States, recently the physical paycheck has been increasingly replaced by electronic direct deposit to bank accounts.

a. Tax expense
b. Total Expense Ratio
c. 3M Company
d. Payroll

Chapter 9. Major Tax Structures: Taxes on Goods and Services

1. _____ consists of the sale of goods or merchandise from a fixed location, such as a department store, boutique or kiosk in small or individual lots for direct consumption by the purchaser. _____ may include subordinated services, such as delivery. Purchasers may be individuals or businesses.

   a. BNSF Railway
   b. Retailing
   c. 3M Company
   d. BMC Software, Inc.

2. _____ refers to the additional value of a commodity over the cost of commodities used to produce it from the previous stage of production. An example is the price of gasoline at the pump over the price of the oil in it. In national accounts used in macroeconomics, it refers to the contribution of the factors of production, i.e., land, labor, and capital goods, to raising the value of a product and corresponds to the incomes received by the owners of these factors.

   a. Value added
   b. Supply-side economics
   c. 3M Company
   d. Minimum wage

3. A _____ is the pinnacle activity involved in selling products or services in return for money or other compensation. It is an act of completion of a commercial activity.

   A _____ is completed by the seller, the owner of the goods.

   a. Sale
   b. Maturity
   c. Tertiary sector of economy
   d. High yield stock

4. An _____ is a type of tax charged on goods produced within the country (as opposed to customs duties, charged on goods from outside the country.) It is a tax on the production or sale of a good.

   Typical examples of excise duties are taxes on tobacco, alcohol and gasoline.

   a. Income tax
   b. Equity of condition
   c. Use tax
   d. Excise tax

Chapter 9. Major Tax Structures: Taxes on Goods and Services

5. _____ laws are laws which attempt to regulate habits of consumption. Black's Law Dictionary defines them as 'Laws made for the purpose of restraining luxury or extravagance, particularly against inordinate expenditures in the matter of apparel, food, furniture, etc.'. Traditionally, they were laws which regulated and reinforced social hierarchies and morals through restrictions on clothing, food, and luxury expenditures.
   a. Robinson-Patman Act
   b. Patent
   c. Joint venture
   d. Sumptuary

6. In economics, an _____ or spillover of an economic transaction is an impact on a party that is not directly involved in the transaction. In such a case, prices do not reflect the full costs or benefits in production or consumption of a product or service. A positive impact is called an external benefit, while a negative impact is called an external cost.
   a. AMEX
   b. AIG
   c. ABC Television Network
   d. Externality

7. _____ is the process of estimation in unknown situations. Prediction is a similar, but more general term. Both can refer to estimation of time series, cross-sectional or longitudinal data.
   a. BMC Software, Inc.
   b. BNSF Railway
   c. 3M Company
   d. Forecasting

8. _____ is any physical or virtual entity that is owned by an individual or jointly by a group of individuals. An owner of _____ has the right to consume, sell, rent, mortgage, transfer and exchange his or her _____. Important widely-recognized types of _____ include real _____, personal _____ (other physical possessions), and intellectual _____ (rights over artistic creations, inventions, etc.), although the latter is not always as widely recognized or enforced.
   a. Disclosure requirement
   b. Property
   c. Fiduciary
   d. Primary authority

9. _____ are the income that is gained by governments because of taxation of the people.

Chapter 9. Major Tax Structures: Taxes on Goods and Services

Just as there are different types of tax, the form in which _____ is collected also differs; furthermore, the agency that collects the tax may not be part of central government, but may be an alternative third-party licenced to collect tax which they themselves will use. For example:

- In the UK, the DVLA collects road tax, which is then passed on the treasury.

_____s on purchases can come from two forms: 'tax' itself is a percentage of the price added to the purchase (such as sales tax in US states, or VAT in the UK), while 'duty' is a fixed amount added to the purchase price (such as is commonly found on cigarettes.) In order to calculate the total tax raised from these sales, we must work out the effective tax rate multiplied by the quantity supplied.

a. Life insurance tax shelter
b. National War Tax Resistance Coordinating Committee
c. Disposable income
d. Tax revenue

10. A _____ is a type of excise tax levied in the United States. It is assessed upon otherwise 'tax free' tangible personal property purchased by a resident of the assessing state for use, storage or consumption of goods in that state (not for resale), regardless of where the purchase took place. The _____ is typically assessed at the same rate as the sales tax that would have been owed (if any) had the same goods been purchased in the state of residence.

a. Use Tax
b. Equity of condition
c. Implied level of government service
d. Income tax

Chapter 10. Major Tax Structures: Property Taxes

1. _____ is any physical or virtual entity that is owned by an individual or jointly by a group of individuals. An owner of _____ has the right to consume, sell, rent, mortgage, transfer and exchange his or her _____. Important widely-recognized types of _____ include real _____, personal _____ (other physical possessions), and intellectual _____ (rights over artistic creations, inventions, etc.), although the latter is not always as widely recognized or enforced.
   a. Primary authority
   b. Fiduciary
   c. Property
   d. Disclosure requirement

2. _____ consists of the sale of goods or merchandise from a fixed location, such as a department store, boutique or kiosk in small or individual lots for direct consumption by the purchaser. _____ may include subordinated services, such as delivery. Purchasers may be individuals or businesses.
   a. 3M Company
   b. BNSF Railway
   c. BMC Software, Inc.
   d. Retailing

3. A _____ is the pinnacle activity involved in selling products or services in return for money or other compensation. It is an act of completion of a commercial activity.

   A _____ is completed by the seller, the owner of the goods.

   a. Maturity
   b. High yield stock
   c. Tertiary sector of economy
   d. Sale

4. In economics, an _____ or spillover of an economic transaction is an impact on a party that is not directly involved in the transaction. In such a case, prices do not reflect the full costs or benefits in production or consumption of a product or service. A positive impact is called an external benefit, while a negative impact is called an external cost.
   a. AIG
   b. AMEX
   c. ABC Television Network
   d. Externality

Chapter 10. Major Tax Structures: Property Taxes

5. _____ is the act of taking possession of or assigning purpose to properties or ideas and is important in many topics, including:

- _____ in relation to the spread of knowledge
- _____ (art)
  - _____ (music) in reference to the re-use and proliferation of different types of music
- _____ (economics) origination of human ownership of previously unowned natural resources such as land
- _____ (law) as a component of government spending
- Cultural _____ is the borrowing, or theft, of an element of cultural expression of one group by another.
- The tort of _____ is one form of invasion of privacy.

a. Appropriation
b. Improvement
c. Annuity
d. Intangible

6. In probability theory and statistics, the index of dispersion, dispersion index, _____ like the coefficient of variation, is a normalized measure of the dispersion of a probability distribution: it is a measure used to quantify whether a set of observed occurrences are relatively clustered or dispersed compared to a standard statistical model.

It is defined as the ratio of the variance $>\sigma^2$ to the mean $>\mu$,

It is also known as the Fano factor, though this latter is sometimes reserved for windowed data (the mean and variance are computed over a subpopulation), where the index of dispersion is the special case where the window is infinite. Windowing data is frequently done: the VMR is frequently computed over various intervals in time or small regions in space, which may be called 'windows', and the resulting statistic called the Fano factor.

a. Coefficient of dispersion
b. BNSF Railway
c. 3M Company
d. BMC Software, Inc.

7. Discounting is a financial mechanism in which a debtor obtains the right to delay payments to a creditor, for a defined period of time, in exchange for a charge or fee. Essentially, the party that owes money in the present purchases the right to delay the payment until some future date. The _____, or charge, is simply the difference between the original amount owed in the present and the amount that has to be paid in the future to settle the debt.

Chapter 10. Major Tax Structures: Property Taxes

a. Discount factor
b. Discount
c. Risk aversion
d. Discounting

8. _____ is a public financing method which has been used for redevelopment and community improvement projects in many countries including the United States for more than 50 years. With federal and state sources for redevelopment generally less available, _____ has become an often-used financing mechanism for municipalities. Similar or related approaches are used elsewhere in the world.
   a. Value capture
   b. 3M Company
   c. BMC Software, Inc.
   d. Tax increment financing

9. Project _____: The project _____ is a prediction of the costs associated with a particular company project. These costs include labor, materials, and other related expenses. The project _____ is often broken down into specific tasks, with task _____s assigned to each.
   a. 3M Company
   b. BMC Software, Inc.
   c. BNSF Railway
   d. Budget

10. An _____ is a tax levied on the financial income of people, corporations, or other legal entities. Various _____ systems exist, with varying degrees of tax incidence. Income taxation can be progressive, proportional, or regressive.
    a. Ordinary income
    b. Implied level of government service
    c. Individual Retirement Arrangement
    d. Income tax

11. _____ is one of the four Ps of the marketing mix. The other three aspects are product, promotion, and place. It is also a key variable in microeconomic price allocation theory.
    a. Pricing
    b. Price
    c. Target costing
    d. Cost-plus pricing

46 Chapter 11. Revenue from User Fees, User Charges, and Sales by Public Monopolies

1. A _____ is the pinnacle activity involved in selling products or services in return for money or other compensation. It is an act of completion of a commercial activity.

   A _____ is completed by the seller, the owner of the goods.

   a. Tertiary sector of economy
   b. Sale
   c. High yield stock
   d. Maturity

2. A _____ is a charge for the use of a product or service.

   A _____ may apply per use of the good or service or charge the user for use of the good or service. The first is a charge for each time while the second is a charge for bulk or time-limited use.

   a. Indirect tax
   b. Association of Real Estate Taxpayers
   c. Optimal tax
   d. User charge

3. _____ is that which is owed; usually referencing assets owed, but the term can also cover moral obligations and other interactions not requiring money. In the case of assets, _____ is a means of using future purchasing power in the present before a summation has been earned. Some companies and corporations use _____ as a part of their overall corporate finance strategy.
   a. Loan
   b. Debenture
   c. Lender
   d. Debt

4. Employment is a contract between two parties, one being the employer and the other being the _____. An _____ may be defined as: 'A person in the service of another under any contract of hire, express or implied, oral or written, where the employer has the power or right to control and direct the _____ in the material details of how the work is to be performed.' Black's Law Dictionary page 471 (5th ed. 1979.)
   a. ABC Television Network
   b. Employee
   c. AMEX
   d. AIG

5. _____ are the income that is gained by governments because of taxation of the people.

Chapter 11. Revenue from User Fees, User Charges, and Sales by Public Monopolies   47

Just as there are different types of tax, the form in which _____ is collected also differs; furthermore, the agency that collects the tax may not be part of central government, but may be an alternative third-party licenced to collect tax which they themselves will use. For example:

- In the UK, the DVLA collects road tax, which is then passed on the treasury.

_____s on purchases can come from two forms: 'tax' itself is a percentage of the price added to the purchase (such as sales tax in US states, or VAT in the UK), while 'duty' is a fixed amount added to the purchase price (such as is commonly found on cigarettes.) In order to calculate the total tax raised from these sales, we must work out the effective tax rate multiplied by the quantity supplied.

a. Disposable income
b. Life insurance tax shelter
c. National War Tax Resistance Coordinating Committee
d. Tax revenue

6. _____ is a common concept in economics, and gives rise to derived concepts such as consumer debt. Generally _____ is defined by opposition to production. But the precise definition can vary because different schools of economists define production quite differently.
   a. Yield
   b. Mitigating Control
   c. Starving the beast
   d. Consumption

7. In economic models, the _____ time frame assumes no fixed factors of production. Firms can enter or leave the marketplace, and the cost (and availability) of land, labor, raw materials, and capital goods can be assumed to vary. In contrast, in the short-run time frame, certain factors are assumed to be fixed, because there is not sufficient time for them to change.
   a. BMC Software, Inc.
   b. Long-run
   c. 3M Company
   d. Short-run

8. _____ is a survey-based economic technique for the valuation of non-market resources, such as environmental preservation or the impact of contamination. While these resources do give people utility, certain aspects of them do not have a market price as they are not directly sold--for example, people receive benefit from a beautiful view of a mountain, but it would be tough to value using price-based models. _____ surveys are one technique which is used to measure these aspects.

a. BMC Software, Inc.
b. BNSF Railway
c. 3M Company
d. Contingent valuation

9. Project _____: The project _____ is a prediction of the costs associated with a particular company project. These costs include labor, materials, and other related expenses. The project _____ is often broken down into specific tasks, with task _____s assigned to each.
    a. BNSF Railway
    b. BMC Software, Inc.
    c. 3M Company
    d. Budget

10. _____, in law and economics, is a form of risk management primarily used to hedge against the risk of a contingent loss. _____ is defined as the equitable transfer of the risk of a loss, from one entity to another, in exchange for a premium, and can be thought of as a guaranteed small loss to prevent a large, possibly devastating loss. An insurer is a company selling the _____; an insured is the person or entity buying the _____.
    a. AMEX
    b. ABC Television Network
    c. Insurance
    d. AIG

Chapter 12. Collecting Taxes

1. To tax is to impose a financial charge or other levy upon a _____ by a state or the functional equivalent of a state.

Taxes are also imposed by many subnational entities. Taxes consist of direct tax or indirect tax, and may be paid in money or as its labour equivalent (often but not always unpaid.)

   a. State tax levels
   b. Taxpayer
   c. Federal Unemployment Tax Act
   d. Tax avoidance

2. In probability theory and statistics, the index of dispersion, dispersion index, _____ like the coefficient of variation, is a normalized measure of the dispersion of a probability distribution: it is a measure used to quantify whether a set of observed occurrences are relatively clustered or dispersed compared to a standard statistical model.

It is defined as the ratio of the variance $>\sigma^2$ to the mean $>\mu$,

It is also known as the Fano factor, though this latter is sometimes reserved for windowed data (the mean and variance are computed over a subpopulation), where the index of dispersion is the special case where the window is infinite. Windowing data is frequently done: the VMR is frequently computed over various intervals in time or small regions in space, which may be called 'windows', and the resulting statistic called the Fano factor.

   a. 3M Company
   b. Coefficient of dispersion
   c. BMC Software, Inc.
   d. BNSF Railway

3. In economic models, the _____ time frame assumes no fixed factors of production. Firms can enter or leave the marketplace, and the cost (and availability) of land, labor, raw materials, and capital goods can be assumed to vary. In contrast, in the short-run time frame, certain factors are assumed to be fixed, because there is not sufficient time for them to change.
   a. Short-run
   b. 3M Company
   c. BMC Software, Inc.
   d. Long-run

50   *Chapter 12. Collecting Taxes*

4. _____ is any physical or virtual entity that is owned by an individual or jointly by a group of individuals. An owner of _____ has the right to consume, sell, rent, mortgage, transfer and exchange his or her _____. Important widely-recognized types of _____ include real _____, personal _____ (other physical possessions), and intellectual _____ (rights over artistic creations, inventions, etc.), although the latter is not always as widely recognized or enforced.
   a. Fiduciary
   b. Primary authority
   c. Property
   d. Disclosure requirement

5. The general definition of an _____ is an evaluation of a person, organization, system, process, project or product. _____s are performed to ascertain the validity and reliability of information; also to provide an assessment of a system's internal control. The goal of an _____ is to express an opinion on the person/organization/system (etc) in question, under evaluation based on work done on a test basis.
   a. Audit
   b. Audit regime
   c. Assurance service
   d. Institute of Chartered Accountants of India

6. In economics, business, retail, and accounting, a _____ is the value of money that has been used up to produce something, and hence is not available for use anymore. In economics, a _____ is an alternative that is given up as a result of a decision. In business, the _____ may be one of acquisition, in which case the amount of money expended to acquire it is counted as _____.
   a. Cost allocation
   b. Cost of quality
   c. Prime cost
   d. Cost

Chapter 13. Revenue Forecasts, Revenue Estimates, and Tax Expenditure Budgets

1. Project _____: The project _____ is a prediction of the costs associated with a particular company project. These costs include labor, materials, and other related expenses. The project _____ is often broken down into specific tasks, with task _____s assigned to each.
   a. 3M Company
   b. BNSF Railway
   c. Budget
   d. BMC Software, Inc.

2. _____ is the calculated approximation of a result which is usable even if input data may be incomplete or uncertain.

   In statistics, see _____ theory, estimator.

   In mathematics, approximation or _____ typically means finding upper or lower bounds of a quantity that cannot readily be computed precisely and is also an educated guess .

   a. AMEX
   b. Estimation
   c. AIG
   d. ABC Television Network

3. _____ is the process of estimation in unknown situations. Prediction is a similar, but more general term. Both can refer to estimation of time series, cross-sectional or longitudinal data.
   a. BMC Software, Inc.
   b. 3M Company
   c. Forecasting
   d. BNSF Railway

4. _____ refers to the additional value of a commodity over the cost of commodities used to produce it from the previous stage of production. An example is the price of gasoline at the pump over the price of the oil in it. In national accounts used in macroeconomics, it refers to the contribution of the factors of production, i.e., land, labor, and capital goods, to raising the value of a product and corresponds to the incomes received by the owners of these factors.
   a. Value added
   b. Supply-side economics
   c. Minimum wage
   d. 3M Company

Chapter 13. Revenue Forecasts, Revenue Estimates, and Tax Expenditure Budgets

5. The general definition of an _____ is an evaluation of a person, organization, system, process, project or product. _____s are performed to ascertain the validity and reliability of information; also to provide an assessment of a system's internal control. The goal of an _____ is to express an opinion on the person/organization/system (etc) in question, under evaluation based on work done on a test basis.
    a. Assurance service
    b. Audit
    c. Audit regime
    d. Institute of Chartered Accountants of India

6. In economics, _____ or _____ goods or real _____ refers to factors of production used to create goods or services that are not themselves significantly consumed (though they may depreciate) in the production process. _____ goods may be acquired with money or financial _____. In finance and accounting, _____ generally refers to financial wealth, especially that used to start or maintain a business.
    a. Disclosure
    b. Vyborg Appeal
    c. Screening
    d. Capital

7. Employment is a contract between two parties, one being the employer and the other being the _____. An _____ may be defined as: 'A person in the service of another under any contract of hire, express or implied, oral or written, where the employer has the power or right to control and direct the _____ in the material details of how the work is to be performed.' Black's Law Dictionary page 471 (5th ed. 1979.)
    a. ABC Television Network
    b. AIG
    c. Employee
    d. AMEX

8. _____ are the income that is gained by governments because of taxation of the people.

Just as there are different types of tax, the form in which _____ is collected also differs; furthermore, the agency that collects the tax may not be part of central government, but may be an alternative third-party licenced to collect tax which they themselves will use. For example:

- In the UK, the DVLA collects road tax, which is then passed on the treasury.

_____s on purchases can come from two forms: 'tax' itself is a percentage of the price added to the purchase (such as sales tax in US states, or VAT in the UK), while 'duty' is a fixed amount added to the purchase price (such as is commonly found on cigarettes.) In order to calculate the total tax raised from these sales, we must work out the effective tax rate multiplied by the quantity supplied.

a. Disposable income
b. Life insurance tax shelter
c. Tax Revenue
d. National War Tax Resistance Coordinating Committee

9. The _____ is a Cabinet-level office, and is the largest office within the Executive Office of the President of the United States (EOP.) It is an important conduit by which the White House oversees the activities of federal agencies. OMB is tasked with giving expert advice to senior White House officials on a range of topics relating to federal policy, management, legislative, regulatory, and budgetary issues.

   a. AT'T Wireless Services, Inc.
   b. Analysis of variance
   c. Alaska Air Group
   d. Office of Management and Budget

10. _____s are statistical models used in econometrics. An _____ specifies the statistical relationship that is believed to hold between the various economic quantities pertaining a particular economic phenomena under study. An _____ can be derived from a deterministic economic model by allowing for uncertainty or from an economic model which itself is stochastic.

    a. ABC Television Network
    b. AIG
    c. AMEX
    d. Econometric model

11. _____ is a system for businesses and individuals to pay installments of their expected tax liability on their income from employment, business, or investment for the current income year.

In Australia, _____ withholding arrangements replaced pay as you earn arrangements when the new tax system was introduced in July 2000. The new arrangements did not confine themselves to employment arrangements and also replaced the Prescribed Payments System and the Reportable Payments System.

   a. Yield
   b. Pay-as-you-go
   c. Residence trusts
   d. Shrinkage

Chapter 13. Revenue Forecasts, Revenue Estimates, and Tax Expenditure Budgets

12. A _____ is any one of a variety of different systems, institutions, procedures, social relations and infrastructures whereby persons trade, and goods and services are exchanged, forming part of the economy. It is an arrangement that allows buyers and sellers to exchange things. _____s vary in size, range, geographic scale, location, types and variety of human communities, as well as the types of goods and services traded.
   a. Perfect competition
   b. Recession
   c. Market
   d. Market Failure

13. _____ was an American statesman and jurist who shaped American constitutional law and made the Supreme Court a center of power. Marshall was Chief Justice of the United States, serving from February 4, 1801, until his death in 1835. He served in the United States House of Representatives from March 4, 1799, to June 7, 1800, and, under President John Adams, was Secretary of State from June 6, 1800, to March 4, 1801.
   a. Alan Greenspan
   b. Arthur Betz Laffer
   c. Abby Joseph Cohen
   d. John Marshall

Chapter 14. Intergovernmental Fiscal Relations: Diversity and Coordination

1. The term _____ refers to government debt, expenditures and revenues, or to finance (particularly financial revenue) in general.

    - _____ deficit is the budget deficit of federal or local government
    - _____ policy is the discretionary spending of governments. Contrasts with monetary policy.
    - _____ year and _____ quarter are reporting periods for firms and other agencies.

See also

    - Procurator _____ and Crown Office and Procurator _____ Service

   a. Comparable
   b. Scientific Research and Experimental Development Tax Incentive Program
   c. Swap
   d. Fiscal

2. Discounting is a financial mechanism in which a debtor obtains the right to delay payments to a creditor, for a defined period of time, in exchange for a charge or fee. Essentially, the party that owes money in the present purchases the right to delay the payment until some future date. The _____, or charge, is simply the difference between the original amount owed in the present and the amount that has to be paid in the future to settle the debt.
   a. Risk aversion
   b. Discount
   c. Discount factor
   d. Discounting

3. _____ are grants, issued by the United States Congress, which may be spent only for narrowly-defined purposes. Additionally, recipients of _____ are often required to match a portion of the federal funds. About 90% of federal aid dollars are spent for _____.
   a. 3M Company
   b. BMC Software, Inc.
   c. Modified Accelerated Cost Recovery System
   d. Categorical grants

4. In a federal system of government, a _____ is a large sum of money granted by the national government to a regional government with only general provisions as to the way it is to be spent. This can be contrasted with a categorical grant which has more strict and specific provisions on the way it is to be spent.

An advantage of a _____ is that they allow regional governments to experiment with different ways of spending money with the same goal in mind, though it is very difficult to compare the results of such spending and reach a conclusion.

a. Block grant
b. 3M Company
c. BMC Software, Inc.
d. BNSF Railway

5. A _____ is the pinnacle activity involved in selling products or services in return for money or other compensation. It is an act of completion of a commercial activity.

A _____ is completed by the seller, the owner of the goods.

a. Tertiary sector of economy
b. Maturity
c. High yield stock
d. Sale

Chapter 15. Debt Administration

1. _____ is that which is owed; usually referencing assets owed, but the term can also cover moral obligations and other interactions not requiring money. In the case of assets, _____ is a means of using future purchasing power in the present before a summation has been earned. Some companies and corporations use _____ as a part of their overall corporate finance strategy.
    a. Lender
    b. Loan
    c. Debenture
    d. Debt

2. In economics, business, retail, and accounting, a _____ is the value of money that has been used up to produce something, and hence is not available for use anymore. In economics, a _____ is an alternative that is given up as a result of a decision. In business, the _____ may be one of acquisition, in which case the amount of money expended to acquire it is counted as _____.
    a. Cost
    b. Prime cost
    c. Cost of quality
    d. Cost allocation

3. A municipality is an administrative entity composed of a clearly defined territory and its population and commonly denotes a city, town or a small grouping of them. A municipality is typically governed by a mayor and a city council or _____ council.

    The notion of municipality includes townships but is not restricted to them.

    a. BNSF Railway
    b. BMC Software, Inc.
    c. 3M Company
    d. Municipal

4. In finance, the term _____ describes the amount in cash that returns to the owners of a security. Normally it does not include the price variations, at the difference of the total return. _____ applies to various stated rates of return on stocks (common and preferred, and convertible), fixed income instruments (bonds, notes, bills, strips, zero coupon), and some other investment type insurance products (e.g. annuities.)
    a. Pension System
    b. Disclosure
    c. Residence trusts
    d. Yield

Chapter 15. Debt Administration

5. In finance, a _____ is a debt security, in which the authorized issuer owes the holders a debt and, depending on the terms of the _____, is obliged to pay interest (the coupon) and/or to repay the principal at a later date, termed maturity. It is a formal contract to repay borrowed money with interest at fixed intervals.

   Thus a _____ is like a loan: the issuer is the borrower, the _____ holder is the lender, and the coupon is the interest.

   a. Revenue bonds
   b. Coupon rate
   c. Bond
   d. Zero-coupon bond

6. An _____ is a bond where the principal is indexed to inflation. They are thus designed to cut out the inflation risk of an investment. The first known _____ was issued by the Massachusetts Bay Company in 1780.
   a. AIG
   b. AMEX
   c. ABC Television Network
   d. Inflation-indexed bond

7. A _____ is a bond issued by a city or other local government, or their agencies. Potential issuers of these include cities, counties, redevelopment agencies, school districts, publicly owned airports and seaports, and any other governmental entity (or group of governments) below the state level. A _____ may be a general obligation of the issuer or secured by specified revenues.
   a. Callable bond
   b. Zero-coupon
   c. Convertible bond
   d. Municipal bond

8. _____ is the process of changing the way taxes are collected or managed by the government.

   _____ers have different goals. Some seek to reduce the level of taxation of all people by the government.

   a. Tax exporting
   b. Tax Reform
   c. Tax investigation
   d. Franchise tax

Chapter 15. Debt Administration

9. The U.S. Congress passed the _____, (Pub.L. 99-514, 100 Stat. 2085, enacted October 22, 1986) to simplify the income tax code, broaden the tax base and eliminate many tax shelters and other preferences.

The tax reform was designed to be revenue neutral, but because individual taxes were decreased while corporate taxes were increased, Congressional Budget Office estimates (which ignore corporate taxes) suggested every tax payer saw a decrease in their tax bill. As of 2009, the _____ was the most recent major simplification of the tax code, drastically reducing the number of deductions and the number of tax brackets.

a. BMC Software, Inc.
b. Tax Reform Act of 1986
c. BNSF Railway
d. 3M Company

10. _____ is any physical or virtual entity that is owned by an individual or jointly by a group of individuals. An owner of _____ has the right to consume, sell, rent, mortgage, transfer and exchange his or her _____. Important widely-recognized types of _____ include real _____, personal _____ (other physical possessions), and intellectual _____ (rights over artistic creations, inventions, etc.), although the latter is not always as widely recognized or enforced.

a. Disclosure requirement
b. Fiduciary
c. Primary authority
d. Property

11. A _____ assesses the credit worthiness of an individual, corporation, or even a country. It is an evaluation made by credit bureaus of a borrower's overall credit history. They are calculated from financial history and current assets and liabilities.

a. Loan
b. Debenture
c. Credit Rating
d. Debt

12. In economics, an _____ or spillover of an economic transaction is an impact on a party that is not directly involved in the transaction. In such a case, prices do not reflect the full costs or benefits in production or consumption of a product or service. A positive impact is called an external benefit, while a negative impact is called an external cost.

a. AMEX
b. AIG
c. Externality
d. ABC Television Network

Chapter 15. Debt Administration

13. _____ refers to the additional value of a commodity over the cost of commodities used to produce it from the previous stage of production. An example is the price of gasoline at the pump over the price of the oil in it. In national accounts used in macroeconomics, it refers to the contribution of the factors of production, i.e., land, labor, and capital goods, to raising the value of a product and corresponds to the incomes received by the owners of these factors.
    a. 3M Company
    b. Supply-side economics
    c. Minimum wage
    d. Value added

14. A standard, commercial _____ is a document issued mostly by a financial institution, used primarily in trade finance, which usually provides an irrevocable payment undertaking.

    The _____ can also be the source of payment for a transaction, meaning that redeeming the _____ will pay an exporter. They are used primarily in international trade transactions of significant value, for deals between a supplier in one country and a customer in another.

    a. Model Code of Professional Responsibility
    b. Lien
    c. Fair Labor Standards Act
    d. Letter of credit

15. _____ is a fee paid on borrowed assets. It is the price paid for the use of borrowed money, or, money earned by deposited funds. Assets that are sometimes lent with _____ include money, shares, consumer goods through hire purchase, major assets such as aircraft, and even entire factories in finance lease arrangements. The _____ is calculated upon the value of the assets in the same manner as upon money.
    a. Interest
    b. Insolvency
    c. AIG
    d. ABC Television Network

16. An _____ is the price a borrower pays for the use of money they do not own, for instance a small company might borrow from a bank to kick start their business, and the return a lender receives for deferring the use of funds, by lending it to the borrower. _____s are normally expressed as a percentage rate over the period of one year.

    _____s targets are also a vital tool of monetary policy and are used to control variables like investment, inflation, and unemployment.

Chapter 15. Debt Administration

a. AIG
b. AMEX
c. ABC Television Network
d. Interest rate

17. _____ is the state or fact of exclusive rights and control over property, which may be an object, land/real estate or intellectual property. An _____ right is also referred to as title.

_____ is the key building block in the development of the capitalist socio-economic system.

a. Administrative proceeding
b. ABC Television Network
c. Ownership
d. Encumbrance

18. All firms can divide the balance sheet into assets and liabilities. For banks the assets are commercial and personal loans, mortgages, construction loans and securities. The liabilities are deposits from customers. The _____ is then the difference between the revenues on the assets and the cost of servicing the liabilities. Notice that both cash flows are not interest payments. In other words, the _____ is the difference between the interest payments to the bank on loans and the interest payments by the bank to the customers on the deposits.
a. Return of capital
b. Yield Gap
c. Sterling ratio
d. Net Interest Income

Chapter 16. Managing Funds: Cash Management and Employee Retirement Funds

1. In United States banking, _____ is a marketing term for certain services offered primarily to larger business customers. It may be used to describe all bank accounts (such as checking accounts) provided to businesses of a certain size, but it is more often used to describe specific services such as cash concentration, zero balance accounting, and automated clearing house facilities. Sometimes, private banking customers are given _____ services.
    a. Profitability index
    b. 3M Company
    c. Finance lease
    d. Cash management

2. Employment is a contract between two parties, one being the employer and the other being the _____. An _____ may be defined as: 'A person in the service of another under any contract of hire, express or implied, oral or written, where the employer has the power or right to control and direct the _____ in the material details of how the work is to be performed.' Black's Law Dictionary page 471 (5th ed. 1979.)
    a. AMEX
    b. Employee
    c. ABC Television Network
    d. AIG

3. _____ is a common concept in economics, and gives rise to derived concepts such as consumer debt. Generally _____ is defined by opposition to production. But the precise definition can vary because different schools of economists define production quite differently.
    a. Mitigating Control
    b. Yield
    c. Starving the beast
    d. Consumption

4. _____ are the income that is gained by governments because of taxation of the people.

Just as there are different types of tax, the form in which _____ is collected also differs; furthermore, the agency that collects the tax may not be part of central government, but may be an alternative third-party licenced to collect tax which they themselves will use. For example:

- In the UK, the DVLA collects road tax, which is then passed on the treasury.

_____s on purchases can come from two forms: 'tax' itself is a percentage of the price added to the purchase (such as sales tax in US states, or VAT in the UK), while 'duty' is a fixed amount added to the purchase price (such as is commonly found on cigarettes.) In order to calculate the total tax raised from these sales, we must work out the effective tax rate multiplied by the quantity supplied.

Chapter 16. Managing Funds: Cash Management and Employee Retirement Funds

a. National War Tax Resistance Coordinating Committee
b. Disposable income
c. Life insurance tax shelter
d. Tax revenue

5. Project _____: The project _____ is a prediction of the costs associated with a particular company project. These costs include labor, materials, and other related expenses. The project _____ is often broken down into specific tasks, with task _____s assigned to each.
   a. 3M Company
   b. BMC Software, Inc.
   c. BNSF Railway
   d. Budget

6. In economics, _____ or _____ goods or real _____ refers to factors of production used to create goods or services that are not themselves significantly consumed (though they may depreciate) in the production process. _____ goods may be acquired with money or financial _____. In finance and accounting, _____ generally refers to financial wealth, especially that used to start or maintain a business.
   a. Vyborg Appeal
   b. Disclosure
   c. Capital
   d. Screening

7. _____ or net present worth (NPW) is defined as the total present value (PV) of a time series of cash flows. It is a standard method for using the time value of money to appraise long-term projects. Used for capital budgeting, and widely throughout economics, it measures the excess or shortfall of cash flows, in present value terms, once financing charges are met.
   a. Present value
   b. Future value
   c. Net present value
   d. 3M Company

8. _____ is the value on a given date of a future payment or series of future payments, discounted to reflect the time value of money and other factors such as investment risk. _____ calculations are widely used in business and economics to provide a means to compare cash flows at different times on a meaningful 'like to like' basis.

The most commonly applied model of the time value of money is compound interest.

Chapter 16. Managing Funds: Cash Management and Employee Retirement Funds

   a. Present value
   b. Net present value
   c. 3M Company
   d. Future value

9. The general definition of an _____ is an evaluation of a person, organization, system, process, project or product. _____s are performed to ascertain the validity and reliability of information; also to provide an assessment of a system's internal control. The goal of an _____ is to express an opinion on the person/organization/system (etc) in question, under evaluation based on work done on a test basis.
   a. Audit regime
   b. Assurance service
   c. Institute of Chartered Accountants of India
   d. Audit

10. _____ is an electronic network for financial transactions in the United States. _____ processes large volumes of both credit and debit transactions, which are originated in batches. Rules and regulations governing the _____ network are established by NAutomated Clearing HouseA-The Electronic Payments Association (formerly the National _____ Association) and the Federal Reserve (Fed.)
   a. AIG
   b. Automated Clearing House
   c. Electronic data interchange
   d. ABC Television Network

11. An _____ is a term used in behavioral economics to describe those types of behaviors that impose costs on a person in the long-run that are not taken into account when making decisions in the present. Classical Economics discourages government from creating legislation that targets internalities, because it is assumed that the consumer takes these personal costs into account when paying for the good that causes the _____. For example, cigarettes should be taxed because of the negative consumption externalities that they impose, such as second-hand smoke, not because the smoker harms him or herself by smoking.
   a. Operating budget
   b. Authorised capital
   c. Inventory turnover ratio
   d. Internality

Chapter 16. Managing Funds: Cash Management and Employee Retirement Funds

12. The _____ is the United States federal government agency that collects taxes and enforces the internal revenue laws. It is an agency within the U.S. Dept of the treasury responsible for interpretation and application of Federal tax law. The official U.S. Treasury regulations provide (in part):

The _____ is a bureau of the Department of the Treasury under the immediate direction of the Commissioner of Internal Revenue.

   a. Income tax
   b. Use tax
   c. Indirect tax
   d. Internal Revenue Service

13. Treasury securities are government debt issued by the United States Department of the Treasury through the Bureau of the Public Debt. They are the debt financing instruments of the U.S. Federal government, and they are often referred to simply as Treasuries or Treasurys. There are four types of marketable treasury securities: _____, Treasury notes, Treasury bonds, and Treasury Inflation Protected Securities (TIPS.)

_____ mature in one year or less. Like zero-coupon bonds, they do not pay interest prior to maturity; instead they are sold at a discount of the par value to create a positive yield to maturity. Many regard _____ as the least risky investment available to U.S. investors.

   a. BNSF Railway
   b. 3M Company
   c. BMC Software, Inc.
   d. Treasury bills

14. A _____ is a time deposit, a financial product commonly offered to consumers by banks, thrift institutions, and credit unions.

They are similar to savings accounts in that they are insured and thus virtually risk-free; they are 'money in the bank' (_____s are insured by the FDIC for banks or by the NCUA for credit unions.) They are different from savings accounts in that the _____ has a specific, fixed term (often three months, six months, or one to five years), and, usually, a fixed interest rate.

Chapter 16. Managing Funds: Cash Management and Employee Retirement Funds

   a. Certificate of deposit
   b. Transactional account
   c. Reserve requirement
   d. Prime rate

15. A _____ is the pinnacle activity involved in selling products or services in return for money or other compensation. It is an act of completion of a commercial activity.

A _____ is completed by the seller, the owner of the goods.

   a. High yield stock
   b. Tertiary sector of economy
   c. Sale
   d. Maturity

16. In the global money market, _____ is an unsecured promissory note with a fixed maturity of one to 270 days. _____ is a money-market security issued (sold) by large banks and corporations to get money to meet short term debt obligations (for example, payroll), and is only backed by an issuing bank or corporation's promise to pay the face amount on the maturity date specified on the note. Since it is not backed by collateral, only firms with excellent credit ratings from a recognized rating agency will be able to sell their _____ at a reasonable price.
   a. Flow-through entity
   b. Commercial paper
   c. Controlling interest
   d. Gross profit margin

17. A _____ allows a borrower to use a financial security as collateral for a cash loan at a fixed rate of interest. In a repo, the borrower agrees to sell immediately a security to a lender and also agrees to buy the same security from the lender at a fixed price at some later date. A repo is equivalent to a cash transaction combined with a forward contract.
   a. BNSF Railway
   b. 3M Company
   c. BMC Software, Inc.
   d. Repurchase agreement

18. _____ is that which is owed; usually referencing assets owed, but the term can also cover moral obligations and other interactions not requiring money. In the case of assets, _____ is a means of using future purchasing power in the present before a summation has been earned. Some companies and corporations use _____ as a part of their overall corporate finance strategy.

Chapter 16. Managing Funds: Cash Management and Employee Retirement Funds

a. Loan
b. Debt
c. Lender
d. Debenture

19. In economics, business, retail, and accounting, a _____ is the value of money that has been used up to produce something, and hence is not available for use anymore. In economics, a _____ is an alternative that is given up as a result of a decision. In business, the _____ may be one of acquisition, in which case the amount of money expended to acquire it is counted as _____.
   a. Prime cost
   b. Cost of quality
   c. Cost allocation
   d. Cost

20. A municipality is an administrative entity composed of a clearly defined territory and its population and commonly denotes a city, town or a small grouping of them. A municipality is typically governed by a mayor and a city council or _____ council.

The notion of municipality includes townships but is not restricted to them.

   a. BNSF Railway
   b. Municipal
   c. 3M Company
   d. BMC Software, Inc.

21. A _____ is a professionally managed type of collective investment scheme that pools money from many investors and invests it in stocks, bonds, short-term money market instruments, and/or other securities. The _____ will have a fund manager that trades the pooled money on a regular basis. As of early 2008, the worldwide value of all _____s totals more than $26 trillion.
   a. Laffer curve
   b. Competition law
   c. Mutual fund
   d. Moving average

22. A _____ is a pool of assets forming an independent legal entity that are bought with the contributions to a pension plan for the exclusive purpose of financing pension plan benefits.

Chapter 16. Managing Funds: Cash Management and Employee Retirement Funds

_____s are important shareholders of listed and private companies. They are especially important to the stock market where large institutional investors like the Ontario Teachers' Pension Plan dominate.

a. Public offering
b. Limited liability company
c. Return on assets
d. Pension fund

23. _____ is any physical or virtual entity that is owned by an individual or jointly by a group of individuals. An owner of _____ has the right to consume, sell, rent, mortgage, transfer and exchange his or her _____. Important widely-recognized types of _____ include real _____, personal _____ (other physical possessions), and intellectual _____ (rights over artistic creations, inventions, etc.), although the latter is not always as widely recognized or enforced.

a. Disclosure requirement
b. Primary authority
c. Fiduciary
d. Property

ANSWER KEY

Chapter 1
1. b 2. b 3. d 4. b 5. a 6. c 7. d 8. d

Chapter 2
1. d 2. d 3. c 4. c 5. d 6. d 7. d 8. c 9. d 10. b
11. d 12. b

Chapter 3
1. d 2. a 3. d 4. d 5. b 6. d 7. c 8. b 9. d 10. a
11. c 12. d 13. d 14. d 15. b 16. b

Chapter 4
1. b 2. c 3. a 4. d 5. c 6. c 7. d 8. a 9. c 10. b
11. b 12. d 13. d 14. a 15. d 16. d 17. b

Chapter 5
1. d 2. a 3. d 4. d 5. d 6. b 7. d 8. d 9. d 10. d
11. d 12. a 13. d

Chapter 6
1. c 2. d 3. d 4. b 5. d 6. c 7. a 8. c 9. d 10. d
11. b 12. d 13. a 14. d 15. a 16. b 17. a 18. d

Chapter 7
1. d 2. b 3. c 4. d 5. d 6. d 7. b 8. c 9. b 10. d
11. c 12. d 13. d

Chapter 8
1. a 2. d 3. c 4. d 5. d 6. d 7. a 8. d 9. d 10. d
11. d 12. d 13. d 14. a 15. d 16. c 17. c 18. c 19. b 20. b
21. a 22. a 23. d 24. b 25. d

Chapter 9
1. b 2. a 3. a 4. d 5. d 6. d 7. d 8. b 9. d 10. a

Chapter 10
1. c 2. d 3. d 4. d 5. a 6. a 7. b 8. d 9. d 10. d
11. a

Chapter 11
1. b 2. d 3. d 4. b 5. d 6. d 7. b 8. d 9. d 10. c

Chapter 12
1. b 2. b 3. d 4. c 5. a 6. d

Chapter 13
1. c 2. b 3. c 4. a 5. b 6. d 7. c 8. c 9. d 10. d
11. b 12. c 13. d

Chapter 14
1. d 2. b 3. d 4. a 5. d

Chapter 15
1. d 2. a 3. d 4. d 5. c 6. d 7. d 8. b 9. b 10. d
11. c 12. c 13. d 14. d 15. a 16. d 17. c 18. d

Chapter 16
1. d 2. b 3. d 4. d 5. d 6. c 7. c 8. a 9. d 10. b
11. d 12. d 13. d 14. a 15. c 16. b 17. d 18. b 19. d 20. b
21. c 22. d 23. d

www.ingramcontent.com/pod-product-compliance
Lightning Source LLC
Chambersburg PA
CBHW081850230426
43669CB00018B/2891